CARNIVORE DIET SLOW COOKER COOKBOOK

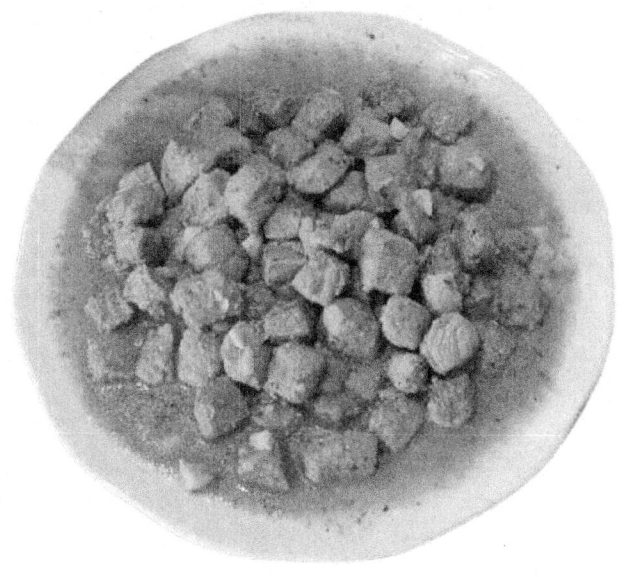

ALEX PEACHEY

Copyright © 2024 by Alex Peachey

All rights reserved.

No part of this publication may be reproduced, stored in a retrieval system, or transmitted, in any form or by any means, electronic, mechanical, photocopying, recording or otherwise, without the prior written permission of the copyright holder.

This book is sold subject to the condition that it shall not, by way of trade or otherwise, be lent, re-sold, hired out or otherwise circulated without the publisher's prior consent in any form of binding or cover other than that in which it is published and without a similar condition including this condition being imposed on the subsequent purchaser.

The author has made every effort to ensure the accuracy and completeness of the Information contained in this book. However, the author and publisher assume no responsibility for errors, inaccuracies, omissions, or any inconsistency herein. Any slights of people, places or organizations are unintentional.

DISCLAIMER

The content within this book reflects my thoughts, experiences, and beliefs. It is meant for informational and entertainment purposes. While I have taken great care to provide accurate information, I cannot guarantee the absolute correctness or applicability of the content to every individual or situation. Please consult with relevant professionals for advice specific to your needs.

TABLE OF CONTENTS

INTRODUCTION 1

CHAPTER 1 6

What is the Carnivore Diet? 6

    Key Principles of the Carnivore Diet: 6

    Benefits of the Carnivore Diet: 7

    Slow Cooking on the Carnivore Diet: 8

CHAPTER 2 10

Getting Started with Slow Cooking 10

    Benefits of Slow Cooking on the Carnivore Diet: 10

    Choosing the Right Slow Cooker 10

    Essential Tools and Ingredients 11

    Tips for Successful Carnivore Slow Cooking 12

CHAPTER 3 14

Beef Recipes 14

    Classic Slow Cooked Beef Roast 14

    Savory Beef Stew 15

    Garlic Butter Beef Tips 16

    Spicy Shredded Beef 17

    Braised Short Ribs 18

    Garlic and Herb Beef Chuck Roast 19

    Herb-Crusted Beef Tri-Tip 20

    Smoky BBQ Beef Ribs 21

    Coffee-Infused Beef Brisket 22

    Mediterranean Beef Kebabs 23

CHAPTER 4 24

Pork Delights 24

    Slow Cooked Pork Shoulder 24

    Crispy Pork Carnitas 25

    Garlic and Herb Pork Chops 26

    Tangy Pulled Pork 27

    Rosemary Infused Pork Loin 28

    Garlic Dijon Pork Tenderloin 29

    Cajun Butter Pork Ribs 30

    Spiced Pork Sirloin Roast 31

    Herb-Infused Pork Butt 32

    Lemon Garlic Pork Loin Chops 33

CHAPTER 5 34

Poultry Pleasures 34

    Herb Roasted Chicken Thighs 34

    Lemon Garlic Turkey Breast 35

    Rosemary Infused Chicken Thighs 36

    Creamy Garlic Chicken Drumsticks 37

    Herb-Crusted Chicken Thighs 38

Lemon Butter Chicken Wings 39

Garlic Butter Turkey Legs 40

Cajun Chicken Thighs 41

Lemon Herb Cornish Hens 42

Garlic Parmesan Chicken Wings 43

CHAPTER 6 44

Seafood Creations 44

Lemon Butter Shrimp Scampi 44

Garlic Herb Butter Lobster Tails 45

Cajun Butter Scallop Skewers 46

Herb-Crusted Salmon Fillets 47

Spicy Garlic Butter Clams 48

Lemon Dill Halibut Steaks 49

Garlic Butter Shrimp Skewers 50

Herb-Infused Tuna Steaks 51

Creamy Garlic Butter Crab Legs 52

Smoked Paprika Salmon Fillets 53

CHAPTER 7 54

Organ Meat Specialties 54

Kidney Stew Delicacy 54

Heartwarming Beef Heart Stew 55

Tongue Tacos Fiesta 56

Lamb Brain Curry 57

Sweet and Sour Pork Kidney 58

Savory Lamb Liver Pâté 59

Beef Tripe Tom Yum Soup 60

Lamb Spleen Stir-Fry 61

Beef Testicles Sauté 62

Braised Lamb Kidneys with Rosemary 63

CHAPTER 8 64

28 DAY MEAL PLAN 64

Week 1: 64

Week 2: 65

Week 3: 67

Week 4: 69

CONCLUSION 71

BONUS CHAPTER 73

10 SNACKS RECIPES 73

Bacon-Wrapped Cheese Bites 73

Beef Jerky Strips 74

Parmesan Crisps 75

Garlic Butter Shrimp Skewers 76

Crispy Pork Rinds 77

Egg and Bacon Bites 78

Spicy Pork Belly Bites 79

Sausage and Cheese Bites 80

Lamb Loin Chops 81

Chicken Liver Pops 82

MEAL PLANNER JOURNAL..**83**

OTHER BOOKS BY THE AUTHOR

CARNIVORE DIET COOKBOOK FOR MEN

CARNIVORE DIET COOKBOOK FOR SENIORS

CARNIVORE DIET COOKBOOK FOR BEGINNERS

CARNIVORE DIET COOKBOOK FOR WOMEN OVER 60

TO SEE THE ABOVE BOOKS SCAN THE QR CODE

INTRODUCTION

In the hustle and bustle of life, our health often takes a back seat, hidden behind the demands of work, family, and the myriad responsibilities that come our way. As Chef Alex Peachey, I found myself caught in this whirlwind, juggling culinary expertise with the pressures of everyday life. Little did I know that my journey would take an unexpected turn towards a remarkable transformation, unlocking the door to a world of health and vitality through the Carnivore Diet.

Let me take you back to a time when I was not the carnivorous chef you know today, but a person struggling with the burden of excess weight and the consequences of a diet that lacked balance. Growing up, I was anything but a Carnivore enthusiast. My childhood was filled with the flavors of diverse cuisines, a melting pot of culinary experiences that shaped my identity as a chef. Yet, despite my love for food, I found myself grappling with the very real challenges of being overweight.

In a world filled with tantalizing temptations and instant gratifications, the consequences of my food choices became evident. As the pounds piled on, I faced the harsh reality of compromised health and a diminishing sense of well-being. I reached a crossroads where I had to confront the impact of my eating habits on my life. It was time for a change, a transformative journey that would lead me to the Carnivore Diet.

The Carnivore Diet, a concept so simple yet profoundly effective, became my beacon of hope. As I delved into the world of Carnivore eating, I discovered a lifestyle that not only shed excess weight but also offered a range of health benefits that went beyond the physical. It was a holistic transformation that touched the very core of my being.

Imagine shedding those extra pounds effortlessly, feeling a surge of energy coursing through your veins, and witnessing a mental clarity that lifts the fog of everyday stresses. These were the gifts the Carnivore Diet bestowed upon me. The carnivorous journey became a revelation, a culinary adventure that rewired my relationship with food and, in turn, my entire life.

As you embark on this journey with me, ask yourself the questions that once echoed in my mind. What if there was a way to eat that not only satisfies your taste buds but also nourishes your body in the most primal way possible? How would it feel to reclaim your health and vitality, break free from the shackles of unhealthy eating habits, and embrace a lifestyle that celebrates the simplicity and power of Carnivore foods?

It's essential to address the dangers and consequences of a diet laden with processed foods, sugars, and additives. The world bombards us with quick fixes and convenience, but at what cost? How many times have we compromised our health for the sake of a fleeting indulgence? The Carnivore Diet, rooted in the ancestral wisdom of our hunter-gatherer ancestors, emerges as a beacon of health in a sea of nutritional confusion.

Chef Alex Peachey, with 25 years of culinary experience, has curated this Carnivore Diet Slow Cooker Cookbook as a testament to the incredible potential within each of us to transform our lives through conscious and intentional eating. This cookbook is more than a collection of recipes; it is a roadmap to vitality, a guide that empowers you to take charge of your health and well-being.

In these pages, you will find not just recipes but a narrative that unfolds the benefits of Carnivore eating. Imagine savoring mouthwatering dishes that not only tantalize your taste buds but also nourish your body with essential nutrients. The Carnivore

Diet, with its emphasis on animal-based foods, is a powerhouse of proteins, healthy fats, and vital nutrients, a combination that fuels your body to perform at its peak.

Beyond the physical benefits, the Carnivore Diet has the potential to become a transformative force in your life. Experience mental clarity that sharpens your focus and a sense of well-being that radiates from within. As Chef Alex Peachey, I invite you to embrace this journey, to savor the flavors of Carnivore eating, and to unlock the doors to a healthier, happier you.

The Carnivore Diet Slow Cooker Cookbook is your companion on this adventure. It combines the efficiency of slow cooking with the power of Carnivore ingredients, making it easier than ever to integrate this lifestyle into your daily routine. Picture the convenience of preparing delicious, nutrient-dense meals with minimal effort, allowing you to savor the richness of life without compromising your health.

As you flip through these pages, let the enticing aroma of slow-cooked Carnivore creations transport you to a world where health and flavor intertwine seamlessly. Chef Alex Peachey, with a friendly tone and a wealth of experience, guides you through each recipe, offering tips and insights that elevate your culinary experience.

My journey from a person struggling with excess weight to the Carnivore Chef has been nothing short of transformative. The Carnivore Diet became my compass, guiding me towards a healthier, more vibrant existence. Now, armed with knowledge, experience, and a passion for culinary excellence, I invite you to join me on this remarkable journey. The Carnivore Diet Slow Cooker Cookbook is not just a collection of recipes; it's a roadmap to a life of abundance, vitality, and flavorful satisfaction. Let the adventure begin.

Contact the Author

Thank you for reading my book! I would love to hear from you, whether you have feedback, questions, or just want to share your thoughts. Your feedback means a lot to me and helps me improve as a writer.

Please don't hesitate to reach out to me through

contactalexpeachey@gmail.com

I look forward to connecting with my readers and appreciate your support in this literary journey. Your thoughts and comments are valuable to me.

CHAPTER 1

WHAT IS THE CARNIVORE DIET?

The Carnivore Diet is a dietary approach that emphasizes the consumption of animal products exclusively, excluding all plant-based foods. Advocates of the Carnivore Diet argue that our ancestors thrived on animal-based nutrition and that eliminating plants can lead to various health benefits. The primary focus is on consuming meat, fish, eggs, and other animal-derived products, while avoiding carbohydrates, fruits, vegetables, and other plant-based sources of nutrition.

Key Principles of the Carnivore Diet:

- **Animal Products Only:** The diet centers around meat, fish, and animal products, with little to no intake of plant-based foods.

- **Elimination of Carbohydrates:** Carbohydrates, including grains, fruits, and vegetables, are excluded to maintain a low-carb, high-fat nutritional profile.

- **Emphasis on Fat:** Healthy fats from animal sources are encouraged, contributing to a high-fat, moderate-protein, and low-carb macronutrient ratio.

- **Bioavailability of Nutrients:** Advocates suggest that animal products provide highly bioavailable forms of essential nutrients, making them easily absorbed by the body.

Benefits of the Carnivorc Diet:

Proponents of the Carnivore Diet claim several potential benefits associated with this way of eating. While scientific research on the long-term effects is limited, some reported benefits include:

Weight Loss and Fat Metabolism:

- **Increased Fat Loss:** The diet's low-carb nature may promote the body's reliance on stored fat for energy, potentially aiding in weight loss.

- **Stabilized Blood Sugar:** By eliminating carbohydrates, some individuals experience stabilized blood sugar levels, reducing cravings and promoting fat burning.

Mental Clarity and Focus:

- **Improved Mental Function:** Supporters argue that a carnivorous diet can enhance mental clarity and focus, attributing it to the elimination of potential brain fog associated with certain plant compounds.

Digestive Health:

- **Reduced Digestive Issues:** For some, removing fiber and plant-based compounds may alleviate digestive discomfort and conditions such as bloating and gas.

Autoimmune and Inflammatory Conditions:

- **Potential Reduction in Inflammation:** Advocates suggest that the diet may mitigate inflammation, potentially benefiting those with autoimmune conditions.

Slow Cooking on the Carnivore Diet:

Slow cooking aligns well with the Carnivore Diet principles, offering a convenient and flavorful way to prepare meat-centric meals. The low-and-slow cooking method enhances tenderness and allows for the infusion of rich flavors without the need for excessive seasonings or additives. It's a practical approach for busy individuals adhering to the Carnivore Diet, providing delicious, nutrient-dense meals with minimal effort. Slow cooking is especially effective for tougher cuts of meat, breaking down collagen and resulting in succulent, melt-in-your-mouth dishes that fit seamlessly into the Carnivore lifestyle.

CHAPTER 2

GETTING STARTED WITH SLOW COOKING

Embarking on your Carnivore Diet journey with slow cooking can enhance the flavors and tenderness of your meat-centric meals. Here's a guide to help you get started:

Benefits of Slow Cooking on the Carnivore Diet:

- **Tenderizes Tough Cuts:** Slow cooking is ideal for tougher cuts of meat, breaking down collagen and connective tissues to achieve a melt-in-your-mouth texture.

- **Enhances Flavor:** The prolonged cooking time allows flavors to meld and intensify, resulting in rich and savory dishes.

- **Convenience:** Set it and forget it! Slow cookers offer a hands-off approach, making meal preparation convenient for busy carnivores.

Choosing the Right Slow Cooker

Selecting the right slow cooker is crucial for successful Carnivore slow cooking. Consider the following factors:

Size and Capacity:

- Choose a size that suits your cooking needs, ensuring it can accommodate the quantity of meat you plan to cook.

- Opt for a larger capacity if you enjoy batch cooking for leftovers.

Temperature Settings:

- Look for a slow cooker with adjustable temperature settings to provide flexibility in cooking different cuts of meat.

Programmable Features:

- A programmable slow cooker allows you to set specific cooking times, ensuring your carnivorous creations are perfectly cooked.

Easy to Clean:

- Consider models with removable, dishwasher-safe parts for hassle-free cleanup.

Essential Tools and Ingredients

Equip your kitchen with the essentials for Carnivore slow cooking success:

Meat Thermometer:

- Ensure accurate cooking by using a meat thermometer to check internal temperatures.

Quality Cuts of Meat:

- Choose high-quality, preferably grass-fed or pasture-raised, cuts of meat for optimal flavor and nutrient content.

Seasonings:

- While the Carnivore Diet emphasizes simplicity, consider using salt, pepper, and carnivore-friendly herbs and spices to enhance flavors.

Cooking Fat:

- Incorporate healthy fats like tallow, lard, or butter for added flavor and to maintain the diet's macronutrient ratios.

Tips for Successful Carnivore Slow Cooking

Make the most of your slow cooking experience with these helpful tips:

Patience is Key:

- Slow cooking is a gradual process; resist the temptation to open the lid frequently to check progress.

Searing for Flavor:

- For an extra layer of flavor, sear meat before placing it in the slow cooker.

Properly Layer Ingredients:

- Place denser, tougher cuts at the bottom of the slow cooker and layer lighter items on top for even cooking.

Adjust Seasonings at the End:

- Taste and adjust seasonings just before serving to ensure a well-balanced flavor profile.

CHAPTER 3

BEEF RECIPES

Classic Slow Cooked Beef Roast

Cooking Time: 8 hours on low

Servings: 6

Ingredients:

- 3 lbs beef roast
- Salt and pepper to taste

Instructions:

1. Season the beef roast with salt and pepper.
2. Place the seasoned roast in the slow cooker.
3. Cook on low for 8 hours.
4. Once done, let it rest for 15 minutes before slicing.
5. Serve slices with cooking juices.

Nutritional Information: Calories: 300 | Carbs: 0g | Protein: 45g | Fat: 12g | Fiber: 0g

Tips:

- Searing the roast before slow cooking enhances flavor.
- Save the cooking juices for a delicious sauce.

Savory Beef Stew

Cooking Time: 6 hours on low

Servings: 8

Ingredients:

- 2 lbs stewing beef
- 4 cups beef broth
- 1 onion, chopped
- 3 cloves garlic, minced
- 4 carrots, sliced
- 2 turnips, diced
- Salt and thyme to taste

Instructions:

1. Combine all ingredients in the slow cooker.
2. Cook on low for 6 hours.
3. Adjust seasoning before serving.

Nutritional Information: Calories: 350 | Carbs: 10g | Protein: 30g | Fat: 20g | Fiber: 3g

Tips:

- Add turnips for a low-carb alternative to potatoes.
- Thicken with xanthan gum if desired.

Garlic Butter Beef Tips

Cooking Time: 4 hours on low

Servings: 4

Ingredients:

- 2 lbs beef tips
- 1/2 cup butter, melted
- 4 cloves garlic, minced
- Salt and parsley to taste

Instructions:

1. Toss beef tips in melted butter and garlic.
2. Place in the slow cooker.
3. Cook on low for 4 hours.
4. Season with salt and parsley before serving.

Nutritional Information: Calories: 400 | Carbs: 1g | Protein: 50g | Fat: 22g | Fiber: 0g

Tips:

- Use grass-fed butter for added richness.
- Serve over cauliflower mash for a complete meal.

Spicy Shredded Beef

Cooking Time: 7 hours on low

Servings: 6

Ingredients:

- 3 lbs beef chuck roast
- 1 cup beef broth
- 1 jalapeño, sliced
- 2 tsp cayenne pepper
- Salt to taste

Instructions:

1. Place beef in the slow cooker, add broth, jalapeño, and cayenne.
2. Cook on low for 7 hours.
3. Shred beef using two forks.
4. Adjust salt before serving.

Nutritional Information: Calories: 280 | Carbs: 2g | Protein: 40g | Fat: 12g | Fiber: 1g

Tips:

- Customize spice level by adjusting cayenne.
- Serve in lettuce wraps for a low-carb option.

Braised Short Ribs

Cooking Time: 6 hours on low

Servings: 4

Ingredients:

- 2 lbs beef short ribs
- 1 cup red wine
- 1 cup beef broth
- 2 cloves garlic, minced
- Salt and rosemary to taste

Instructions:

1. Season short ribs with salt and place in the slow cooker.
2. Mix wine, broth, and garlic; pour over ribs.
3. Cook on low for 6 hours.
4. Sprinkle with rosemary before serving.

Nutritional Information: Calories: 450 | Carbs: 4g | Protein: 35g | Fat: 30g | Fiber: 0g

Tips:

- Use a dry red wine for a richer flavor.
- Skim excess fat before serving.

Garlic and Herb Beef Chuck Roast

Cooking Time: 8 hours on low

Servings: 6

Ingredients:

- 3 lbs beef chuck roast
- 6 cloves garlic, minced
- 2 tbsp fresh rosemary, chopped
- Salt and black pepper to taste

Instructions:

1. Rub the chuck roast with minced garlic, rosemary, salt, and pepper.
2. Place the seasoned roast in the slow cooker.
3. Cook on low for 8 hours.
4. Allow the roast to rest for 15 minutes before slicing.
5. Serve with the aromatic cooking juices.

Nutritional Information: Calories: 320 | Carbs: 2g | Protein: 45g | Fat: 15g | Fiber: 0g

Tips:

- Add a splash of bone broth for extra richness.
- Serve with sautéed spinach for a nutrient boost.

Herb-Crusted Beef Tri-Tip

Cooking Time: 5 hours on low

Servings: 4

Ingredients:

- 2 lbs beef tri-tip
- 3 tbsp fresh thyme, chopped
- 2 tbsp fresh oregano, chopped
- 4 cloves garlic, minced
- Salt and olive oil

Instructions:

1. Mix thyme, oregano, garlic, salt, and enough olive oil to form a paste.
2. Rub the tri-tip with the herb paste.
3. Place the tri-tip in the slow cooker.
4. Cook on low for 5 hours.
5. Slice and serve with the herb-infused cooking juices.

Nutritional Information: Calories: 380 | Carbs: 1g | Protein: 50g | Fat: 18g | Fiber: 0g

Tips:

- Sear the tri-tip before slow cooking for added flavor.
- Use the cooking juices to make a simple au jus.

Smoky BBQ Beef Ribs

Cooking Time: 6 hours on low

Servings: 4

Ingredients:

- 2 lbs beef back ribs
- 1 cup sugar-free BBQ sauce
- 2 tsp smoked paprika
- Salt and black pepper to taste

Instructions:

1. Rub ribs with smoked paprika, salt, and pepper.
2. Place ribs in the slow cooker and pour BBQ sauce over them.
3. Cook on low for 6 hours.
4. Baste with cooking juices before serving.

Nutritional Information: Calories: 420 | Carbs: 5g | Protein: 35g | Fat: 28g | Fiber: 1g

Tips:

- Check the ingredients of the BBQ sauce for hidden sugars.
- Finish under the broiler for a caramelized crust.

Coffee-Infused Beef Brisket

Cooking Time: 10 hours on low

Servings: 8

Ingredients:

- 4 lbs beef brisket
- 2 cups strong black coffee
- 3 tbsp smoked sea salt
- 2 tbsp ground black pepper

Instructions:

1. Season brisket with smoked sea salt and black pepper.
2. Place brisket in the slow cooker and pour black coffee over it.
3. Cook on low for 10 hours.
4. Slice and serve with the coffee-infused juices.

Nutritional Information: Calories: 350 | Carbs: 0g | Protein: 45g | Fat: 18g | Fiber: 0g

Tips:

- Use a bold coffee for a robust flavor.
- Save leftover brisket for delicious carnivore-friendly sandwiches.

Mediterranean Beef Kebabs

Cooking Time: 4 hours on low

Servings: 4

Ingredients:

- 2 lbs beef stew meat, cubed
- 1/4 cup olive oil
- 2 tbsp fresh oregano, chopped
- 1 tbsp lemon juice
- Salt and black pepper to taste

Instructions:

1. In a bowl, mix olive oil, oregano, lemon juice, salt, and pepper.
2. Coat the beef cubes in the marinade.
3. Skewer the beef cubes and place in the slow cooker.
4. Cook on low for 4 hours.
5. Serve with a squeeze of fresh lemon.

Nutritional Information: Calories: 320 | Carbs: 1g | Protein: 50g | Fat: 14g | Fiber: 0g

Tips:

- Soak skewers in water before use to prevent burning.
- Pair with a side of grilled zucchini for a complete meal.

CHAPTER 4

PORK DELIGHTS

Slow Cooked Pork Shoulder

Cooking Time: 8 hours on low

Servings: 6

Ingredients:

- 4 lbs pork shoulder
- Salt and black pepper to taste

Instructions:

1. Season the pork shoulder with salt and pepper.
2. Place the seasoned pork in the slow cooker.
3. Cook on low for 8 hours.
4. Shred the pork and serve with its juices.

Nutritional Information: Calories: 400 | Carbs: 0g | Protein: 50g | Fat: 22g | Fiber: 0g

Tips:

- Sear the pork before slow cooking for a caramelized exterior.
- Use the leftover juices to make a flavorful sauce.

Crispy Pork Carnitas

Cooking Time: 6 hours on low

Servings: 8

Ingredients:

- 3 lbs pork loin
- 1 cup lard or tallow
- 2 tsp ground cumin
- Salt and oregano to taste

Instructions:

1. Cut pork into chunks and season with cumin, salt, and oregano.
2. Place the pork in the slow cooker and cover with melted lard or tallow.
3. Cook on low for 6 hours.
4. Shred and crisp up the carnitas under the broiler before serving.

Nutritional Information: Calories: 350 | Carbs: 0g | Protein: 45g | Fat: 18g | Fiber: 0g

Tips:

- Use a mix of lard and tallow for added richness.
- Serve carnitas in lettuce wraps for a low-carb option.

Garlic and Herb Pork Chops

Cooking Time: 4 hours on low

Servings: 4

Ingredients:

- 4 pork chops
- 6 cloves garlic, minced
- 2 tbsp fresh thyme, chopped
- Salt and black pepper to taste

Instructions:

1. Rub pork chops with minced garlic, thyme, salt, and pepper.
2. Place the seasoned chops in the slow cooker.
3. Cook on low for 4 hours.
4. Serve with the aromatic cooking juices.

Nutritional Information: Calories: 300 | Carbs: 0g | Protein: 40g | Fat: 15g | Fiber: 0g

Tips:

- Searing the pork chops before slow cooking enhances flavor.
- Add a splash of bone broth for extra richness.

Tangy Pulled Pork

Cooking Time: 7 hours on low

Servings: 6

Ingredients:

- 3 lbs pork butt
- 1 cup apple cider vinegar
- 2 tbsp mustard powder
- Salt and paprika to taste

Instructions:

1. Season pork butt with mustard powder, salt, and paprika.
2. Place the pork in the slow cooker and pour apple cider vinegar over it.
3. Cook on low for 7 hours.
4. Shred and serve with a tangy vinegar-based sauce.

Nutritional Information: Calories: 380 | Carbs: 0g | Protein: 50g | Fat: 20g | Fiber: 0g

Tips:

- Adjust the level of tanginess by varying the vinegar amount.
- Serve on a bed of cabbage for a refreshing crunch.

Rosemary Infused Pork Loin

Cooking Time: 5 hours on low

Servings: 4

Ingredients:

- 2 lbs pork loin
- 3 tbsp fresh rosemary, chopped
- 4 cloves garlic, minced
- Salt and black pepper to taste

Instructions:

1. Mix chopped rosemary, minced garlic, salt, and pepper.
2. Rub the mixture onto the pork loin.
3. Place the pork in the slow cooker.
4. Cook on low for 5 hours.
5. Slice and serve with the infused cooking juices.

Nutritional Information: Calories: 320 | Carbs: 0g | Protein: 45g | Fat: 15g | Fiber: 0g

Tips:

- Use a meat thermometer to ensure proper cooking.
- Add a touch of lemon for a citrusy twist.

Garlic Dijon Pork Tenderloin

Cooking Time: 4 hours on low

Servings: 4

Ingredients:

- 2 lbs pork tenderloin
- 4 cloves garlic, minced
- 3 tbsp Dijon mustard
- Salt and black pepper to taste

Instructions:

1. Combine minced garlic, Dijon mustard, salt, and pepper.
2. Rub the mixture onto the pork tenderloin.
3. Place the tenderloin in the slow cooker.
4. Cook on low for 4 hours.
5. Slice and serve with the flavorful cooking juices.

Nutritional Information: Calories: 280 | Carbs: 2g | Protein: 40g | Fat: 12g | Fiber: 0g

Tips:

- Add a touch of fresh thyme for an extra herbal note.
- Baste the tenderloin with the cooking juices during cooking.

Cajun Butter Pork Ribs

Cooking Time: 6 hours on low

Servings: 4

Ingredients:

- 2 lbs pork ribs
- 1/2 cup unsalted butter, melted
- 2 tbsp Cajun seasoning
- Salt to taste

Instructions:

1. Coat pork ribs with melted butter and Cajun seasoning.
2. Place the ribs in the slow cooker.
3. Cook on low for 6 hours.
4. Season with salt before serving.

Nutritional Information: Calories: 450 | Carbs: 1g | Protein: 30g | Fat: 35g | Fiber: 0g

Tips:

- Adjust Cajun seasoning to your preferred spice level.
- Finish under the broiler for a crispy exterior.

Spiced Pork Sirloin Roast

Cooking Time: 5 hours on low

Servings: 6

Ingredients:

- 3 lbs pork sirloin roast
- 2 tsp ground coriander
- 1 tsp smoked paprika
- Salt and black pepper to taste

Instructions:

1. Rub pork sirloin with ground coriander, smoked paprika, salt, and pepper.
2. Place the roast in the slow cooker.
3. Cook on low for 5 hours.
4. Slice and serve with the spiced cooking juices.

Nutritional Information: Calories: 320 | Carbs: 0g | Protein: 45g | Fat: 15g | Fiber: 0g

Tips:

- Let the roast rest before slicing for juicier meat.
- Use the leftover juices as a base for a hearty soup.

Herb-Infused Pork Butt

Cooking Time: 8 hours on low

Servings: 8

Ingredients:

- 4 lbs pork butt
- 4 tbsp fresh sage, chopped
- 2 tbsp fresh thyme, chopped
- Salt and black pepper to taste

Instructions:

1. Mix chopped sage, thyme, salt, and pepper.
2. Rub the mixture onto the pork butt.
3. Place the pork in the slow cooker.
4. Cook on low for 8 hours.
5. Shred and serve with the herb-infused cooking juices.

Nutritional Information: Calories: 380 | Carbs: 0g | Protein: 50g | Fat: 20g | Fiber: 0g

Tips:

- Use a variety of fresh herbs for a complex flavor profile.
- Serve over cauliflower rice for a complete meal.

Lemon Garlic Pork Loin Chops

Cooking Time: 4 hours on low

Servings: 4

Ingredients:

- 1.5 lbs pork loin chops
- 4 cloves garlic, minced
- Zest and juice of 1 lemon
- Salt and black pepper to taste

Instructions:

1. Combine minced garlic, lemon zest, lemon juice, salt, and pepper.
2. Rub the mixture onto the pork loin chops.
3. Place the chops in the slow cooker.
4. Cook on low for 4 hours.
5. Serve with the zesty cooking juices.

Nutritional Information: Calories: 280 | Carbs: 1g | Protein: 35g | Fat: 15g | Fiber: 0g

Tips:

- Marinate the chops for an hour before slow cooking for enhanced flavor.
- Finish with a sprinkle of fresh parsley for brightness.

CHAPTER 5

POULTRY PLEASURES

Herb Roasted Chicken Thighs

Cooking Time: 4 hours on low

Servings: 4

Ingredients:

- 8 chicken thighs
- 3 tbsp fresh rosemary, chopped
- 2 tbsp fresh thyme, chopped

Instructions:

1. Rub chicken thighs with chopped rosemary, thyme, salt, and pepper.
2. Place the thighs in the slow cooker.
3. Cook on low for 4 hours.
4. Serve with the herb-infused cooking juices.

Nutritional Information: Calories: 400 | Carbs: 0g | Protein: 50g | Fat: 22g | Fiber: 0g

Tips:

- Searing the chicken thighs before slow cooking enhances flavor.
- Add a squeeze of lemon before serving for brightness.

Lemon Garlic Turkey Breast

Cooking Time: 5 hours on low

Servings: 6

Ingredients:

- 3 lbs turkey breast
- 4 cloves garlic, minced
- Zest and juice of 2 lemons
- Salt and black pepper to taste

Instructions:

1. Combine minced garlic, lemon zest, lemon juice, salt, and pepper.
2. Rub the mixture onto the turkey breast.
3. Place the breast in the slow cooker.
4. Cook on low for 5 hours.
5. Serve with the zesty cooking juices.

Nutritional Information: Calories: 320 | Carbs: 2g | Protein: 45g | Fat: 15g | Fiber: 0g

Tips:

- Baste the turkey breast with the cooking juices during cooking.
- Let the breast rest before slicing for juicier meat.

Rosemary Infused Chicken Thighs

Cooking Time: 4 hours on low

Servings: 4

Ingredients:

- 8 chicken thighs
- 4 tbsp fresh rosemary, chopped
- 3 cloves garlic, minced
- Salt and black pepper to taste

Instructions:

1. Mix chopped rosemary, minced garlic, salt, and pepper.
2. Rub the mixture onto the chicken thighs.
3. Place the thighs in the slow cooker.
4. Cook on low for 4 hours.
5. Serve with the aromatic cooking juices.

Nutritional Information: Calories: 380 | Carbs: 0g | Protein: 50g | Fat: 18g | Fiber: 0g

Tips:

- Use bone-in, skin-on thighs for extra flavor.
- Finish under the broiler for crispy skin.

Creamy Garlic Chicken Drumsticks

Cooking Time: 6 hours on low

Servings: 6

Ingredients:

- 12 chicken drumsticks
- 1 cup heavy cream
- 4 cloves garlic, minced
- Salt and black pepper to taste

Instructions:

1. Season drumsticks with minced garlic, salt, and pepper.
2. Place the drumsticks in the slow cooker and pour heavy cream over them.
3. Cook on low for 6 hours.
4. Serve with the creamy garlic sauce.

Nutritional Information: Calories: 450 | Carbs: 2g | Protein: 40g | Fat: 30g | Fiber: 0g

Tips:

- Add a splash of broth for a thinner sauce.
- Garnish with fresh parsley for color and flavor.

Herb-Crusted Chicken Thighs

Cooking Time: 4 hours on low

Servings: 4

Ingredients:

- 8 chicken thighs
- 3 tbsp fresh thyme, chopped
- 2 tbsp fresh oregano, chopped
- Salt and black pepper to taste

Instructions:

1. Rub chicken thighs with chopped thyme, oregano, salt, and pepper.
2. Place the thighs in the slow cooker.
3. Cook on low for 4 hours.
4. Serve with the herb-infused cooking juices.

Nutritional Information: Calories: 380 | Carbs: 0g | Protein: 50g | Fat: 18g | Fiber: 0g

Tips:

- Use a mix of fresh herbs for a more complex flavor.
- Save the bones for making homemade broth.

Lemon Butter Chicken Wings

Cooking Time: 3 hours on low

Servings: 4

Ingredients:

- 2 lbs chicken wings
- 1/2 cup unsalted butter, melted
- Zest and juice of 2 lemons
- Salt and black pepper to taste

Instructions:

1. Toss chicken wings in melted butter, lemon zest, lemon juice, salt, and pepper.
2. Place the wings in the slow cooker.
3. Cook on low for 3 hours.
4. Serve with the tangy lemon butter sauce.

Nutritional Information: Calories: 420 | Carbs: 1g | Protein: 35g | Fat: 30g | Fiber: 0g

Tips:

- Finish under the broiler for crispy skin.
- Garnish with fresh lemon slices for presentation.

Garlic Butter Turkey Legs

Cooking Time: 6 hours on low

Servings: 4

Ingredients:

- 4 turkey legs
- 1/2 cup unsalted butter, melted
- 6 cloves garlic, minced
- Salt and black pepper to taste

Instructions:

1. Coat turkey legs with melted butter, minced garlic, salt, and pepper.
2. Place the legs in the slow cooker.
3. Cook on low for 6 hours.
4. Baste with cooking juices before serving.

Nutritional Information: Calories: 400 | Carbs: 0g | Protein: 45g | Fat: 22g | Fiber: 0g

Tips:

- Use garlic-infused butter for an extra punch.
- Save the cooking juices for a tasty gravy.

Cajun Chicken Thighs

Cooking Time: 5 hours on low

Servings: 4

Ingredients:

- 8 chicken thighs
- 2 tbsp Cajun seasoning
- Salt to taste

Instructions:

1. Rub chicken thighs with Cajun seasoning and salt.
2. Place the thighs in the slow cooker.
3. Cook on low for 5 hours.
4. Serve with the flavorful cooking juices.

Nutritional Information: Calories: 380 | Carbs: 0g | Protein: 50g | Fat: 18g | Fiber: 0g

Tips:

- Adjust Cajun seasoning to your preferred spice level.
- Serve with a side of sautéed spinach.

Lemon Herb Cornish Hens

Cooking Time: 4 hours on low

Servings: 2

Ingredients:

- 2 Cornish hens
- Zest and juice of 1 lemon
- 3 tbsp fresh thyme, chopped
- Salt and black pepper to taste

Instructions:

1. Rub Cornish hens with lemon zest, lemon juice, chopped thyme, salt, and pepper.
2. Place the hens in the slow cooker.
3. Cook on low for 4 hours.
4. Serve with the herb-infused cooking juices.

Nutritional Information: Calories: 500 | Carbs: 0g | Protein: 60g | Fat: 26g | Fiber: 0g

Tips:

- Roast under the broiler for a crispy skin.
- Garnish with additional fresh thyme for a burst of color.

Garlic Parmesan Chicken Wings

Cooking Time: 3 hours on low

Servings: 4

Ingredients:

- 2 lbs chicken wings
- 1 cup grated Parmesan cheese
- 6 cloves garlic, minced
- Salt and black pepper to taste

Instructions:

1. Toss chicken wings in grated Parmesan cheese, minced garlic, salt, and pepper.
2. Place the wings in the slow cooker.
3. Cook on low for 3 hours.
4. Serve with the cheesy garlic coating.

Nutritional Information: Calories: 450 | Carbs: 1g | Protein: 35g | Fat: 30g | Fiber: 0g

Tips:

- Finish under the broiler for a golden crust.
- Sprinkle extra Parmesan before serving for a decadent touch.

CHAPTER 6

SEAFOOD CREATIONS

Lemon Butter Shrimp Scampi

Cooking Time: 2 hours on low

Servings: 4

Ingredients:

- 2 lbs shrimp, peeled and deveined
- 1/2 cup unsalted butter, melted
- Zest and juice of 2 lemons

Instructions:

1. Toss shrimp in melted butter, lemon zest, lemon juice, salt, and pepper.
2. Place the shrimp in the slow cooker.
3. Cook on low for 2 hours.
4. Serve with the lemon butter sauce.

Nutritional Information: Calories: 350 | Carbs: 2g | Protein: 45g | Fat: 18g | Fiber: 0g

Tips:

- Cook just until shrimp turn pink to avoid overcooking.
- Garnish with fresh parsley for a burst of color.

Garlic Herb Butter Lobster Tails

Cooking Time: 1.5 hours on low

Servings: 2

Ingredients:

- 2 lobster tails, split
- 1/2 cup unsalted butter, melted
- 4 cloves garlic, minced
- Salt and black pepper to taste

Instructions:

1. Coat lobster tails with melted butter, minced garlic, salt, and pepper.
2. Place the tails in the slow cooker.
3. Cook on low for 1.5 hours.
4. Serve with the herb-infused butter.

Nutritional Information: Calories: 400 | Carbs: 1g | Protein: 30g | Fat: 30g | Fiber: 0g

Tips:

- Baste lobster tails with butter during cooking.
- Broil for a minute after slow cooking for a golden finish.

Cajun Butter Scallop Skewers

Cooking Time: 1 hour on low

Servings: 4

Ingredients:

- 1 lb scallops
- 1/2 cup unsalted butter, melted
- 2 tbsp Cajun seasoning
- Salt to taste

Instructions:

1. Toss scallops in melted butter, Cajun seasoning, and salt.
2. Skewer the scallops and place in the slow cooker.
3. Cook on low for 1 hour.
4. Serve with the Cajun butter sauce.

Nutritional Information: Calories: 300 | Carbs: 1g | Protein: 25g | Fat: 20g | Fiber: 0g

Tips:

- Use large scallops for even cooking.
- Soak skewers in water before use to prevent burning.

Herb-Crusted Salmon Fillets

Cooking Time: 2 hours on low

Servings: 4

Ingredients:

- 4 salmon fillets
- 3 tbsp fresh dill, chopped
- 2 tbsp fresh parsley, chopped
- Salt and black pepper to taste

Instructions:

1. Rub salmon fillets with chopped dill, parsley, salt, and pepper.
2. Place the fillets in the slow cooker.
3. Cook on low for 2 hours.
4. Serve with the herb-infused cooking juices.

Nutritional Information: Calories: 450 | Carbs: 0g | Protein: 60g | Fat: 22g | Fiber: 0g

Tips:

- Choose skin-on salmon for added flavor.
- Garnish with a wedge of lemon before serving.

Spicy Garlic Butter Clams

Cooking Time: 1.5 hours on low

Servings: 4

Ingredients:

- 2 lbs clams, cleaned
- 1/2 cup unsalted butter, melted
- 4 cloves garlic, minced
- 2 tsp red pepper flakes
- Salt to taste

Instructions:

1. Toss clams in melted butter, minced garlic, red pepper flakes, and salt.
2. Place the clams in the slow cooker.
3. Cook on low for 1.5 hours.
4. Serve with the spicy garlic butter sauce.

Nutritional Information: Calories: 350 | Carbs: 2g | Protein: 40g | Fat: 18g | Fiber: 0g

Tips:

- Discard any unopened clams after cooking.
- Finish with a sprinkle of fresh parsley for freshness.

Lemon Dill Halibut Steaks

Cooking Time: 2 hours on low

Servings: 4

Ingredients:

- 4 halibut steaks
- Zest and juice of 2 lemons
- 3 tbsp fresh dill, chopped
- Salt and black pepper to taste

Instructions:

1. Rub halibut steaks with lemon zest, lemon juice, chopped dill, salt, and pepper.
2. Place the steaks in the slow cooker.
3. Cook on low for 2 hours.
4. Serve with the lemon dill-infused cooking juices.

Nutritional Information: Calories: 380 | Carbs: 1g | Protein: 45g | Fat: 20g | Fiber: 0g

Tips:

- Check for doneness by flaking the fish with a fork.
- Drizzle extra lemon juice before serving for brightness.

Garlic Butter Shrimp Skewers

Cooking Time: 1 hour on low

Servings: 4

Ingredients:

- 1 lb large shrimp, peeled and deveined
- 1/2 cup unsalted butter, melted
- 6 cloves garlic, minced
- Salt and black pepper to taste

Instructions:

1. Toss shrimp in melted butter, minced garlic, salt, and pepper.
2. Skewer the shrimp and place in the slow cooker.
3. Cook on low for 1 hour.
4. Serve with the garlic butter sauce.

Nutritional Information: Calories: 300 | Carbs: 2g | Protein: 35g | Fat: 18g | Fiber: 0g

Tips:

- Use metal skewers for easier handling.
- Squeeze fresh lemon over the shrimp before serving.

Herb-Infused Tuna Steaks

Cooking Time: 1.5 hours on low

Servings: 4

Ingredients:

- 4 tuna steaks
- 4 tbsp fresh basil, chopped
- 2 tbsp fresh thyme, chopped
- Salt and black pepper to taste

Instructions:

1. Rub tuna steaks with chopped basil, thyme, salt, and pepper.
2. Place the steaks in the slow cooker.
3. Cook on low for 1.5 hours.
4. Serve with the herb-infused cooking juices.

Nutritional Information: Calories: 350 | Carbs: 0g | Protein: 50g | Fat: 18g | Fiber: 0g

Tips:

- Sear the tuna steaks before slow cooking for a crust.
- Sprinkle with sea salt for added flavor.

Creamy Garlic Butter Crab Legs

Cooking Time: 2 hours on low

Servings: 4

Ingredients:

- 2 lbs crab legs
- 1/2 cup unsalted butter, melted
- 6 cloves garlic, minced
- Salt and black pepper to taste

Instructions:

1. Toss crab legs in melted butter, minced garlic, salt, and pepper.
2. Place the crab legs in the slow cooker.
3. Cook on low for 2 hours.
4. Serve with the creamy garlic butter sauce.

Nutritional Information: Calories: 400 | Carbs: 0g | Protein: 40g | Fat: 25g | Fiber: 0g

Tips:

- Crack the crab legs before serving for easier consumption.
- Use a nutcracker to access the succulent meat inside.

Smoked Paprika Salmon Fillets

Cooking Time: 1.5 hours on low

Servings: 4

Ingredients:

- 4 salmon fillets
- 2 tsp smoked paprika
- 4 tbsp olive oil
- Salt and black pepper to taste

Instructions:

1. Rub salmon fillets with smoked paprika, olive oil, salt, and pepper.
2. Place the fillets in the slow cooker.
3. Cook on low for 1.5 hours.
4. Serve with the smoky-flavored cooking juices.

Nutritional Information: Calories: 450 | Carbs: 0g | Protein: 60g | Fat: 22g | Fiber: 0g

Tips:

- Finish under the broiler for a caramelized crust.
- Pair with a side of sautéed spinach for a complete meal.

CHAPTER 7

ORGAN MEAT SPECIALTIES

Kidney Stew Delicacy

Cooking Time: 6 hours on low

Servings: 6

Ingredients:

- 1.5 lbs beef or lamb kidneys, diced
- 2 cups beef bone broth
- 4 cloves garlic, minced

Instructions:

1. Rinse kidneys and pat dry, then sear until browned.
2. Place kidneys in the slow cooker, add bone broth, and minced garlic.
3. Cook on low for 6 hours.
4. Season with salt and pepper before serving.

Nutritional Information: Calories: 250 | Carbs: 2g | Protein: 35g | Fat: 12g | Fiber: 0g

Tips:

- Soaking kidneys in water with a splash of vinegar can reduce the gamey taste.
- Serve over cauliflower rice for a complete meal.

Heartwarming Beef Heart Stew

Cooking Time: 8 hours on low

Servings: 8

Ingredients:

- 2 lbs beef heart, cubed
- 3 cups beef broth
- 2 carrots, sliced
- 2 celery stalks, chopped
- Salt and black pepper to taste

Instructions:

1. Sear beef heart cubes until browned.
2. Place heart, carrots, celery, and broth in the slow cooker.
3. Cook on low for 8 hours.
4. Season with salt and pepper before serving.

Nutritional Information: Calories: 280 | Carbs: 5g | Protein: 40g | Fat: 10g | Fiber: 2g

Tips:

- Trim any visible fat from the beef heart before cooking.
- Experiment with different herbs for added flavor.

Tongue Tacos Fiesta

Cooking Time: 7 hours on low

Servings: 6

Ingredients:

- 2 lbs beef tongue
- 1 onion, sliced
- 3 cloves garlic, minced
- 2 tsp cumin
- Salt and black pepper to taste
- Lettuce leaves for serving

Instructions:

1. Boil beef tongue for 10 minutes, peel skin, then sear until browned.
2. Place tongue, sliced onion, minced garlic, and cumin in the slow cooker.
3. Cook on low for 7 hours.
4. Season with salt and pepper, then serve in lettuce leaves.

Nutritional Information: Calories: 350 | Carbs: 3g | Protein: 45g | Fat: 15g | Fiber: 1g

Tips:

- Add a squeeze of lime for extra freshness.
- Top with salsa or guacamole for additional flavor.

Lamb Brain Curry

Cooking Time: 3 hours on low

Servings: 4

Ingredients:

- 4 lamb brains
- 1 cup coconut milk
- 1 onion, finely chopped
- 2 tbsp curry powder
- Salt to taste

Instructions:

1. Soak lamb brains in cold water for 30 minutes.
2. Mix coconut milk, chopped onion, and curry powder in the slow cooker.
3. Add drained lamb brains and cook on low for 3 hours.
4. Season with salt before serving.

Nutritional Information: Calories: 320 | Carbs: 4g | Protein: 25g | Fat: 22g | Fiber: 1g

Tips:

- Serve over cauliflower rice for a low-carb option.
- Garnish with fresh cilantro for a burst of flavor.

Sweet and Sour Pork Kidney

Cooking Time: 5 hours on low

Servings: 4

Ingredients:

- 1.5 lbs pork kidneys, sliced
- 1/2 cup apple cider vinegar
- 1/4 cup coconut aminos
- 2 tbsp tomato paste
- Salt and black pepper to taste

Instructions:

1. Sear pork kidneys until browned.
2. Place kidneys, apple cider vinegar, coconut aminos, and tomato paste in the slow cooker.
3. Cook on low for 5 hours.
4. Season with salt and pepper before serving.

Nutritional Information: Calories: 280 | Carbs: 5g | Protein: 30g | Fat: 15g | Fiber: 1g

Tips:

- Adjust sweetness with a pinch of stevia or erythritol.
- Serve with sautéed cabbage for a balanced meal.

Savory Lamb Liver Pâté

Cooking Time: 3 hours on low

Servings: 8

Ingredients:

- 1 lb lamb liver
- 1 cup beef tallow
- 3 cloves garlic, minced
- 1 tsp thyme
- Salt and black pepper to taste

Instructions:

1. Sear lamb liver until browned.
2. Place liver, beef tallow, minced garlic, and thyme in the slow cooker.
3. Cook on low for 3 hours.
4. Season with salt and pepper, then blend into a pâté.

Nutritional Information: Calories: 200 | Carbs: 2g | Protein: 25g | Fat: 10g | Fiber: 0g

Tips:

- Spread on cucumber slices for a low-carb snack.
- Refrigerate for a few hours before serving for better consistency.

Beef Tripe Tom Yum Soup

Cooking Time: 6 hours on low

Servings: 6

Ingredients:

- 1 lb beef tripe, cleaned and sliced
- 4 cups beef bone broth
- 2 lemongrass stalks, smashed
- 4 kaffir lime leaves
- Salt and chili flakes to taste

Instructions:

1. Boil beef tripe for 15 minutes, then sear until browned.
2. Place tripe, bone broth, lemongrass, and kaffir lime leaves in the slow cooker.
3. Cook on low for 6 hours.
4. Season with salt and chili flakes before serving.

Nutritional Information: Calories: 230 | Carbs: 3g | Protein: 30g | Fat: 10g | Fiber: 0g

Tips:

- Add fish sauce for an extra umami kick.
- Top with fresh cilantro for brightness.

Lamb Spleen Stir-Fry

Cooking Time: 4 hours on low

Servings: 4

Ingredients:

- 1.5 lbs lamb spleen, sliced
- 1/4 cup coconut oil
- 2 bell peppers, sliced
- 3 cloves garlic, minced
- Salt and black pepper to taste

Instructions:

1. Sear lamb spleen until browned.
2. Place spleen, coconut oil, sliced bell peppers, and minced garlic in the slow cooker.
3. Cook on low for 4 hours.
4. Season with salt and pepper before serving.

Nutritional Information: Calories: 260 | Carbs: 4g | Protein: 30g | Fat: 14g | Fiber: 1g

Tips:

- Add a splash of coconut aminos for a hint of sweetness.
- Serve over zucchini noodles for a low-carb option.

Beef Testicles Sauté

Cooking Time: 3 hours on low

Servings: 4

Ingredients:

- 1 lb beef testicles, sliced
- 1/4 cup ghee or beef tallow
- 2 tsp rosemary, chopped
- 2 tsp thyme, chopped
- Salt and black pepper to taste

Instructions:

1. Blanch beef testicles in boiling water for 5 minutes, then sear until browned.
2. Place testicles, ghee or tallow, chopped rosemary, and thyme in the slow cooker.
3. Cook on low for 3 hours.
4. Season with salt and pepper before serving.

Nutritional Information: Calories: 280 | Carbs: 2g | Protein: 30g | Fat: 18g | Fiber: 0g

Tips:

- Serve with a squeeze of lemon for freshness.
- Pair with a side of sautéed mushrooms for added flavor.

Braised Lamb Kidneys with Rosemary

Cooking Time: 4 hours on low

Servings: 4

Ingredients:

- 1.5 lbs lamb kidneys, halved
- 1 cup beef broth
- 3 tbsp rosemary, chopped
- 4 cloves garlic, minced
- Salt and black pepper to taste

Instructions:

1. Sear lamb kidneys until browned.
2. Place kidneys, beef broth, chopped rosemary, and minced garlic in the slow cooker.
3. Cook on low for 4 hours.
4. Season with salt and pepper before serving.

Nutritional Information: Calories: 260 | Carbs: 3g | Protein: 35g | Fat: 12g | Fiber: 1g

Tips:

- Remove any white connective tissue from kidneys before cooking.
- Garnish with fresh rosemary for a fragrant finish.

CHAPTER 8

28 DAY MEAL PLAN

Week 1:

Day 1:

- **Breakfast:** Bacon-Wrapped Cheese Bites
- **Lunch:** Beef Jerky Strips
- **Dinner:** Parmesan Crisps

Day 2:

- **Breakfast:** Crispy Pork Rinds
- **Lunch:** Egg and Bacon Bites
- **Dinner:** Garlic Butter Shrimp Skewers

Day 3:

- **Breakfast:** Sausage and Cheese Bites
- **Lunch:** Spicy Pork Belly Bites
- **Dinner:** Chicken Liver Pops

Day 4:

- **Breakfast:** Liver Delight
- **Lunch:** Tongue Tacos Fiesta
- **Dinner:** Beef Tripe Tom Yum Soup

Day 5:

- **Breakfast:** Lamb Brain Curry
- **Lunch:** Sweet and Sour Pork Kidney
- **Dinner:** Beef Testicles Sauté

Day 6:

- **Breakfast:** Kidney Stew Delicacy
- **Lunch:** Heartwarming Beef Heart Stew
- **Dinner:** Lamb Spleen Stir-Fry

Day 7:

- **Breakfast:** Liver Delight
- **Lunch:** Tongue Tacos Fiesta
- **Dinner:** Beef Tripe Tom Yum Soup

Week 2:

Day 8:

- **Breakfast:** Lamb Brain Curry
- **Lunch:** Sweet and Sour Pork Kidney
- **Dinner:** Beef Testicles Sauté

Day 9:

- **Breakfast:** Kidney Stew Delicacy
- **Lunch:** Heartwarming Beef Heart Stew
- **Dinner:** Lamb Spleen Stir-Fry

Day 10:

- **Breakfast:** Liver Delight
- **Lunch:** Tongue Tacos Fiesta
- **Dinner:** Beef Tripe Tom Yum Soup

Day 11:

- **Breakfast:** Lamb Brain Curry
- **Lunch:** Sweet and Sour Pork Kidney
- **Dinner:** Beef Testicles Sauté

Day 12:

- **Breakfast:** Kidney Stew Delicacy
- **Lunch:** Heartwarming Beef Heart Stew
- **Dinner:** Lamb Spleen Stir-Fry

Day 13:

- **Breakfast:** Liver Delight
- **Lunch:** Tongue Tacos Fiesta
- **Dinner:** Beef Tripe Tom Yum Soup

Day 14:

- **Breakfast:** Lamb Brain Curry
- **Lunch:** Sweet and Sour Pork Kidney
- **Dinner:** Beef Testicles Sauté

Week 3:

Day 15:

- **Breakfast:** Kidney Stew Delicacy
- **Lunch:** Heartwarming Beef Heart Stew
- **Dinner:** Lamb Spleen Stir-Fry

Day 16:

- **Breakfast:** Liver Delight
- **Lunch:** Tongue Tacos Fiesta
- **Dinner:** Beef Tripe Tom Yum Soup

Day 17:

- **Breakfast:** Lamb Brain Curry
- **Lunch:** Sweet and Sour Pork Kidney
- **Dinner:** Beef Testicles Sauté

Day 18:

- **Breakfast:** Kidney Stew Delicacy
- **Lunch:** Heartwarming Beef Heart Stew
- **Dinner:** Lamb Spleen Stir-Fry

Day 19:

- **Breakfast:** Liver Delight
- **Lunch:** Tongue Tacos Fiesta
- **Dinner:** Beef Tripe Tom Yum Soup

Day 20:

- **Breakfast:** Lamb Brain Curry
- **Lunch:** Sweet and Sour Pork Kidney
- **Dinner:** Beef Testicles Sauté

Day 21:

- **Breakfast:** Kidney Stew Delicacy
- **Lunch:** Heartwarming Beef Heart Stew
- **Dinner:** Lamb Spleen Stir-Fry

Week 4:

Day 22:

- **Breakfast:** Liver Delight
- **Lunch:** Tongue Tacos Fiesta
- **Dinner:** Beef Tripe Tom Yum Soup

Day 23:

- **Breakfast:** Lamb Brain Curry
- **Lunch:** Sweet and Sour Pork Kidney
- **Dinner:** Beef Testicles Sauté

Day 24:

- **Breakfast:** Kidney Stew Delicacy
- **Lunch:** Heartwarming Beef Heart Stew
- **Dinner:** Lamb Spleen Stir-Fry

Day 25:

- **Breakfast:** Liver Delight
- **Lunch:** Tongue Tacos Fiesta
- **Dinner:** Beef Tripe Tom Yum Soup

Day 26:

- **Breakfast:** Lamb Brain Curry
- **Lunch:** Sweet and Sour Pork Kidney
- **Dinner:** Beef Testicles Sauté

Day 27:

- **Breakfast:** Kidney Stew Delicacy
- **Lunch:** Heartwarming Beef Heart Stew
- **Dinner:** Lamb Spleen Stir-Fry

Day 28:

- **Breakfast:** Liver Delight
- **Lunch:** Tongue Tacos Fiesta
- **Dinner:** Beef Tripe Tom Yum Soup

CONCLUSION

As we come to the conclusion of this culinary adventure, I want to express my deepest gratitude for allowing me to share my journey with you. The Carnivore Diet Slow Cooker Cookbook is more than a collection of recipes; it's a testament to the transformative power of intentional eating, a celebration of flavors that not only tantalize the taste buds but also nourish the body and soul.

As Chef Alex Peachey, my mission is to guide you towards a life of vitality and well-being. The Carnivore Diet has been a beacon of hope for me, and it is my sincerest wish that it becomes a source of inspiration and positive change in your life as well.

I invite you to dive into the recipes, savor the flavors, and embrace the simplicity and power of Carnivore eating. Let the slow cooker become your ally in this journey, a tool that effortlessly integrates this lifestyle into your daily routine. Feel the surge of energy, experience mental clarity, and witness the transformation unfold in your life.

Your feedback is invaluable to me. I encourage you to share your thoughts, experiences, and honest reviews. Your insights not only help me improve and refine my offerings but also contribute to a community of individuals committed to optimal health and well-being.

As you embark on this Carnivore journey, remember that you are not alone. Chef Alex Peachey and the Carnivore Diet Slow Cooker Cookbook community are here to support you every step of the way. Share your successes, ask questions, and be a part of a community that celebrates the power of intentional eating.

Thank you for entrusting me with a part of your culinary journey. May the Carnivore Diet bring you joy, health, and a renewed sense of vitality. Here's to your well-being and the delicious adventures that lie ahead.

BONUS CHAPTER

10 SNACKS RECIPES

Bacon-Wrapped Cheese Bites

Cooking Time: 2 hours on low

Servings: 4

Ingredients:

- 16 small cubes of cheese (cheddar or gouda)
- 8 slices of bacon, cut in half

Instructions:

1. Wrap each cheese cube with a half-slice of bacon.
2. Secure with toothpicks and place in the slow cooker.
3. Cook on low for 2 hours until bacon is crispy.

Nutritional Information: Calories: 300 | Carbs: 1g | Protein: 20g | Fat: 25g | Fiber: 0g

Tips:

- Use toothpicks to easily serve these savory bites.
- Broil for a few minutes after slow cooking for extra crispiness.

Beef Jerky Strips

Cooking Time: 4 hours on low

Servings: Varies

Ingredients:

- 1 lb beef sirloin or eye of round, thinly sliced
- 1/2 cup soy sauce or coconut aminos
- 2 tsp garlic powder
- 1 tsp onion powder

Instructions:

1. Marinate beef slices in soy sauce or coconut aminos, garlic powder, and onion powder for 1 hour.
2. Place slices in the slow cooker and cook on low for 4 hours.

Nutritional Information: Calories: 350 | Carbs: 2g | Protein: 50g | Fat: 15g | Fiber: 0g

Tips:

- Slice against the grain for a tender jerky.
- Adjust seasoning to your taste preference.

Parmesan Crisps

Cooking Time: 1.5 hours on low

Servings: Varies

Ingredients:

- 1 cup grated Parmesan cheese

Instructions:

1. Drop small heaps of Parmesan cheese on a lined slow cooker.
2. Cook on low for 1.5 hours until edges are golden and crispy.

Nutritional Information: Calories: 400 | Carbs: 2g | Protein: 40g | Fat: 25g | Fiber: 0g

Tips:

- Add a pinch of black pepper for extra flavor.
- Allow crisps to cool before serving for maximum crispiness.

Garlic Butter Shrimp Skewers

Cooking Time: 1 hour on low

Servings: 4

Ingredients:

- 1 lb large shrimp, peeled and deveined
- 1/2 cup unsalted butter, melted
- 6 cloves garlic, minced
- Salt and black pepper to taste

Instructions:

1. Toss shrimp in melted butter, minced garlic, salt, and pepper.
2. Skewer the shrimp and place in the slow cooker.
3. Cook on low for 1 hour.

Nutritional Information: Calories: 300 | Carbs: 2g | Protein: 35g | Fat: 18g | Fiber: 0g

Tips:

- Use metal skewers for easier handling.
- Squeeze fresh lemon over the shrimp before serving.

Crispy Pork Rinds

Cooking Time: 4 hours on low

Servings: Varies

Ingredients:

- Pork skin (from pork belly or pork shoulder)
- Salt to taste

Instructions:

1. Cut pork skin into bite-sized pieces.
2. Place in the slow cooker and cook on low for 4 hours until crispy.
3. Season with salt.

Nutritional Information: Calories: 200 | Carbs: 0g | Protein: 20g | Fat: 15g | Fiber: 0g

Tips:

- Ensure pork skin is thoroughly dried before cooking.
- Experiment with different seasonings like paprika or cayenne.

Egg and Bacon Bites

Cooking Time: 2 hours on low

Servings: 6

Ingredients:

- 6 hard-boiled eggs, peeled
- 12 slices of bacon, cooked
- Salt and black pepper to taste

Instructions:

1. Wrap each hard-boiled egg with a slice of bacon.
2. Secure with toothpicks and place in the slow cooker.
3. Cook on low for 2 hours until bacon is crispy.

Nutritional Information: Calories: 350 | Carbs: 1g | Protein: 20g | Fat: 30g | Fiber: 0g

Tips:

- Serve with a side of mustard for added flavor.
- Use toothpicks for easy serving.

Spicy Pork Belly Bites

Cooking Time: 3 hours on low

Servings: 4

Ingredients:

- 1 lb pork belly, cubed
- 2 tbsp hot sauce
- 1 tsp garlic powder
- Salt to taste

Instructions:

1. Toss pork belly cubes in hot sauce, garlic powder, and salt.
2. Place in the slow cooker and cook on low for 3 hours.

Nutritional Information: Calories: 450 | Carbs: 1g | Protein: 20g | Fat: 40g | Fiber: 0g

Tips:

- Adjust hot sauce to your preferred spice level.
- Broil for a few minutes after slow cooking for extra crispiness.

Sausage and Cheese Bites

Cooking Time: 2 hours on low

Servings: 4

Ingredients:

- 1 lb sausage links, cooked and sliced
- 1 cup cheddar cheese, cubed

Instructions:

1. Skewer a slice of sausage followed by a cube of cheddar cheese.
2. Place on the slow cooker and cook on low for 2 hours.

Nutritional Information: Calories: 400 | Carbs: 2g | Protein: 25g | Fat: 30g | Fiber: 0g

Tips:

- Use pre-cooked sausage for quicker preparation.
- Serve with mustard or your favorite dipping sauce.

Lamb Loin Chops

Cooking Time: 3 hours on low

Servings: 4

Ingredients:

- 4 lamb loin chops
- 2 tbsp olive oil
- 2 tsp rosemary, chopped
- Salt and black pepper to taste

Instructions:

1. Rub lamb loin chops with olive oil, chopped rosemary, salt, and pepper.
2. Place in the slow cooker and cook on low for 3 hours.

Nutritional Information: Calories: 400 | Carbs: 0g | Protein: 40g | Fat: 25g | Fiber: 0g

Tips:

- Sear the chops before slow cooking for a caramelized crust.
- Serve with a side of mint sauce for freshness.

Chicken Liver Pops

Cooking Time: 2 hours on low

Servings: 4

Ingredients:

- 1 lb chicken livers
- 1/2 cup ghee or beef tallow
- 2 tsp thyme, chopped
- Salt and black pepper to taste

Instructions:

1. Sear chicken livers until browned.
2. Place livers, ghee or tallow, chopped thyme, salt, and pepper in the slow cooker.
3. Cook on low for 2 hours.

Nutritional Information: Calories: 300 | Carbs: 1g | Protein: 35g | Fat: 18g | Fiber: 0g

Tips:

- Soak chicken livers in milk for an hour before cooking.
- Serve with toothpicks for easy snacking.

MEAL PLANNER JOURNAL

WEEKLY PLANNER WEEK _____

Monday

Tuesday

Wednesday

Thursday

Friday

Saturday

Sunday

To Do List
- [ ] _____
- [ ] _____
- [ ] _____
- [ ] _____
- [ ] _____
- [ ] _____
- [ ] _____
- [ ] _____
- [ ] _____
- [ ] _____
- [ ] _____

Notes

WEEKLY PLANNER

WEEK _____

Monday

Tuesday

Wednesday

Thursday

Friday

Saturday

Sunday

To Do List
- ☐ _____
- ☐ _____
- ☐ _____
- ☐ _____
- ☐ _____
- ☐ _____
- ☐ _____
- ☐ _____
- ☐ _____
- ☐ _____
- ☐ _____

Notes

WEEKLY PLANNER

WEEK _____

Monday

Tuesday

Wednesday

Thursday

Friday

Saturday

Sunday

To Do List
- ☐ _____
- ☐ _____
- ☐ _____
- ☐ _____
- ☐ _____
- ☐ _____
- ☐ _____
- ☐ _____
- ☐ _____
- ☐ _____
- ☐ _____
- ☐ _____

Notes

WEEKLY PLANNER

WEEK _____

Monday

Tuesday

Wednesday

Thursday

Friday

Saturday

Sunday

To Do List

☐ _____
☐ _____
☐ _____
☐ _____
☐ _____
☐ _____
☐ _____
☐ _____
☐ _____
☐ _____
☐ _____
☐ _____

Notes

WEEKLY PLANNER

WEEK _____

Monday

Tuesday

Wednesday

Thursday

Friday

Saturday

Sunday

To Do List

- ☐ _____
- ☐ _____
- ☐ _____
- ☐ _____
- ☐ _____
- ☐ _____
- ☐ _____
- ☐ _____
- ☐ _____
- ☐ _____
- ☐ _____
- ☐ _____

Notes

WEEKLY PLANNER

WEEK _____

Monday

Tuesday

Wednesday

Thursday

Friday

Saturday

Sunday

To Do List

☐ _____
☐ _____
☐ _____
☐ _____
☐ _____
☐ _____
☐ _____
☐ _____
☐ _____
☐ _____
☐ _____

Notes

WEEKLY PLANNER

WEEK _____

Monday

Tuesday

Wednesday

Thursday

Friday

Saturday

Sunday

To Do List
- ☐ _____
- ☐ _____
- ☐ _____
- ☐ _____
- ☐ _____
- ☐ _____
- ☐ _____
- ☐ _____
- ☐ _____
- ☐ _____
- ☐ _____
- ☐ _____

Notes

WEEKLY PLANNER

WEEK _____

Monday

Tuesday

Wednesday

Thursday

Friday

Saturday

Sunday

To Do List
- ☐ _____
- ☐ _____
- ☐ _____
- ☐ _____
- ☐ _____
- ☐ _____
- ☐ _____
- ☐ _____
- ☐ _____
- ☐ _____
- ☐ _____
- ☐ _____

Notes

WEEKLY PLANNER

WEEK _____

Monday

Tuesday

Wednesday

Thursday

Friday

Saturday

Sunday

To Do List
- ☐ _____
- ☐ _____
- ☐ _____
- ☐ _____
- ☐ _____
- ☐ _____
- ☐ _____
- ☐ _____
- ☐ _____
- ☐ _____
- ☐ _____
- ☐ _____

Notes

WEEKLY PLANNER

WEEK _____

Monday

Tuesday

Wednesday

Thursday

Friday

Saturday

Sunday

To Do List
- ☐ _____
- ☐ _____
- ☐ _____
- ☐ _____
- ☐ _____
- ☐ _____
- ☐ _____
- ☐ _____
- ☐ _____
- ☐ _____
- ☐ _____
- ☐ _____

Notes

Printed in Great Britain
by Amazon